PAST & PRESENT

CAMARILLO

David Reel

Dad, I dedicate this, my first book, to you. You instilled a love of history, geography, and home in me for which I am deeply grateful. I love you very much, and you will always be deeply missed.

Library of Congress Control Number: 2019940807

Published by Arcadia Publishing
Charleston, South Carolina

Printed in the United States of America

For all general information, please contact Arcadia Publishing:
Telephone 843-853-2070
Fax 843-853-0044
E-mail sales@arcadiapublishing.com
For customer service and orders:
Toll-Free 1-888-313-2665

Visit us on the Internet at www.arcadiapublishing.com

On the Front Cover: The c. 1966 image of the Camarillo Ranch House was taken not long after a Catholic order of Augustinians was gifted the Victorian from Carmen Camarillo. (Past image, courtesy of the Marvel family; present image, courtesy of David Reel.)

On the Back Cover: This July 20, 1924, picture perfectly displays the expansive and elaborate parties the Camarillo family threw for the public to commemorate happy and special occasions. (Courtesy of the Marvel family.)

CONTENTS

ACKNOWLEDGMENTS

First, I thank my wife and best friend, Catherine, without whom the completion of this book would not have been possible. Thanks for all your help, patience, support, and dedication. You are the keeper of my magic, and any idea of life without you is pure fantasy. I love you, girl.

Second, but providing invaluable aid, I thank Ynez Parker LaDow and Carmela LaDow—you two wonderful ladies went to bat for me and got me out of a tight spot, and I am very grateful for it. Theresa and Thomas Marvel, it was wonderful to chat with you. Thank you so much for your help and blessings. Ruth Ann Cawelti and Rhett Searcy, thanks for taking the time to allow me to see your personal albums. Shirley Granger and Betty-Jo Carnes—I appreciate you allowing me to use your pictures, too.

I have a secret fantastic resource that has helped me so much. She has wished to remain anonymous, and I promised I would honor her wish. However, you know who you are, and I thank you.

The last six years have been very tumultuous, and the reasons being are private. That said, I always felt that two of the most important things in life are laughter and friendship. You know who you are, but I will mention you anyway: Wayne Scott, Paul Githens, John Baumann, Josh "Potato" McDonald, Nick "Italian Stallion" Giacopuzzi, Chris Zeller, John Baltes, Pliny Mier, Jeff McVicker, Lori McVicker, John Cox, John Spohn, and Jeff Hahn—you all are such wonderful friends. Your moral support has been invaluable.

Unless otherwise noted, all present images are courtesy of the author.

INTRODUCTION

Camarillo was officially incorporated as a city in 1964, but its history goes all the way back to November 15, 1875, when a 10-year-long chain of events ended with a decree issued by the court in which it was adjudged that Juan Camarillo Sr. become the sole owner of Rancho Calleguas—one of the last Mexican land grants in the state of California. In all, he paid $36,950 for a little over 10,000 acres that his oldest son, Adolfo, inherited in 1880 immediately after Juan Camarillo Sr.'s death.

Rancho Calleguas began as a cattle operation, but everything changed when local farmer Joseph Lewis planted the first lima bean in Ventura County in Camarillo in 1899. At the time, the sugar beet was the "big dog" crop in Ventura County, but the lima bean was different—*much* different. The sugar beet required water, and local farmers depended almost entirely on rain, which, in Ventura County, can often be scarce. The lima bean requires very little water, and although on lush rainy years the sugar beet paid more dividends than the lima bean, the lima bean was a far steadier crop because it did not depend entirely on Mother Nature.

Another important element in Camarillo history occurred in 1899: the Southern Pacific Railroad had just laid tracks on the very western edge of Rancho Calleguas. Adolfo Camarillo had recently built a store with a section for a post office for local merchant John Sebastian west of the tracks and on the main road that went to both Los Angeles and Ventura. The post office needed an official name for the community, and Sebastian sent in the name Calleguas. The post office declined, claiming it was too difficult to pronounce. Sebastian consulted with Adolfo Camarillo, who was pleased to have the post office use his name, which the post office accepted.

In 1901, Adolfo Camarillo formed a partnership with Joseph Lewis, which lasted until 1906. By 1913, the lima bean surpassed the sugar beet as the chief cash crop of Ventura County—75 percent of the world's lima beans came from Ventura County, a large portion of which from Camarillo.

Although he was under five feet in stature, Adolfo Camarillo was sharp and innovative; in addition to the lima bean, he incorporated walnuts, corn, citrus, barley, and hay into his operation. He raised his own cattle, hogs, vegetables, and fruits, and he had his own well for water. When the Great Depression hit and much of the country suffered, Rancho Calleguas never missed a beat; it was completely self-sustaining, and no government help was ever needed or asked for.

In addition to working his property, Adolfo Camarillo was highly active in the community. He was vice president of the First National Bank of Ventura, vice president of the Ojai State Bank of Nordhoff, and a stockholder of both the First National Bank of Oxnard and the Fillmore State Bank in Ventura County. Here is a partial list of a few more of the local organizations in which he served the community: Native Sons of the Golden West, 1888–1958; Pleasant Valley School District Board of Trustees, 1895–1951 (president, 1914–1951); Knights of Columbus (Santa Barbara and Oxnard) as charter member, 1903–1958 (Grand Knight, 1910–1911); cofounder and director of Bank of A. Levy, 1903–1958; Ventura County Board of Supervisors, 1907–1915; Peoples Lumber Company Board of Directors, 1907–1958 (president, 1940–1956); Ventura County Fair Board, 1915–1952 (president, 1915–1946); Oxnard Elks

Lodge, 1922–1958; Ivy Lawn Memorial Park Board of Directors, 1923–1958 (director and president); and California State Fair Board of Directors, 1932–1943.

From a cattle operation to lima beans, Camarillo has made substantial agricultural progress in the last 120 years. Surrounded by mountains on three sides and the Pacific Ocean on the other, Camarillo sits on the northern edge of what is known as the Oxnard Plain, which is a 200-square-mile alluvial plain that contains rich soil, adequate water, and a favorable climate that gives the region a year-round growing season for multiple crops, including strawberries, celery, cabbage, tomatoes, lettuce, raspberries, nursery stock, artichokes, lemons, oranges, avocados, and corn.

For decades, development in Camarillo proceeded slowly, but with the advent of the 101 Freeway in 1954, which bisected the city, the stage was set for an ensuing period of growth. In 1962, the 3M Corporation chose the city as the home of its Mincom and Magnetic Tape Divisions. In 1964, Camarillo became incorporated. Home to Oxnard Air Force Base between 1951 and 1969 and just a few miles from naval bases in Point Mugu and Port Hueneme, Camarillo became a prime spot for many ex-military to settle and raise a family. Today, Camarillo is an attractive bedroom community combining easy proximity with nearby industry and a semirural living environment with a population of approximately 70,000.

Many people consider the Mediterranean climate along the French Riviera to be the best climate in the world, yet Camarillo boasts slightly cooler summers and warmer winters. In August, Nice, France, has an average high temperature of 82 degrees and an average low of 69. August in Camarillo has an average high of 80 and an average low of 60. January is the coldest month in Nice, with an average high of 56 degrees and an average low of 42. December is the coolest month in Camarillo with an average high of 65 and an average low of 42. Thus, if you used a line graph to compare the two climates over a 12-month period, Camarillo's line graph would have less of a curve than that of Nice, France.

CHAPTER 1

VENTURA BOULEVARD AND 101 HIGHWAY

This east-facing aerial view really shows how small Camarillo was back in 1945. The tall building with the steeple at center is St. Mary Magdalen Catholic Chapel, which is located on Ventura Boulevard. The street running parallel with Ventura Boulevard to the left (north) was called Davenport Street, which was removed—along with all the homes on it—in 1953 when construction on the 101 Freeway began. (Courtesy of Jeff Hahn.)

The c. 1939 picture below of downtown Camarillo was taken from the top of the bell tower at St. Mary Magdalen Catholic Chapel. Facing northeast, one is looking straight down Somis Road. Ventura Boulevard intersects Somis Road and crosses the railroad tracks. The flagpole, just below and to the right of the eucalyptus trees, was located in the center of the town square, which was known as the Triangle. To the right of the flagpole is the depot in its original location. (Below, courtesy of the Marvel family.)

PAST & PRESENT

CAMARILLO

Hope you enjoy!

David Peel

OPPOSITE: This northeast-facing shot of downtown Camarillo was taken from the bell tower of the St. Mary Magdalen Catholic Chapel in 1939. The depot is still in its original location some 14 years prior to being moved due to the installation of the 101 Freeway, which began in 1953 and was completed in March 1954. (Courtesy of the Marvel family.)

The St. Mary Magdalen Catholic Chapel was built in July 1914 by the city's founder, Adolfo Camarillo, and his brother Juan to honor their parents. The brothers named the chapel after their oldest sister, Magdalena. The chapel's first service was performed on November 11, 1914—the marriage ceremony of Rosa Camarillo, Adolfo's daughter, to Alfred Petit. The photograph above was taken on July 20, 1924. (Above, courtesy of Pleasant Valley Museum.)

The above photograph is a c. 1900 picture of Ventura Boulevard facing east. The building on the right is J.L. Sebastian's general store. Built in 1899, this was the first business in Camarillo. Sebastian's store was originally a few miles to the west in a community called Springville, but when Adolfo Camarillo got word that the railroad would be coming through Camarillo, he had Sebastian relocate. In addition to selling general supplies and feed, the store also served as a post office, with J.L. Sebastian as the first postmaster of Camarillo. (Above, courtesy of Pleasant Valley Museum.)

In the 1920 image below of Ventura Boulevard facing west, one can easily see St. Mary Magdalen Catholic Chapel watching over the town. At the foot of the chapel—the third building from the left in this picture—is Camarillo's original Catholic chapel, which served the community prior to St. Mary Magdalen being built in 1914. (Below, courtesy of John Spohn.)

Juan Camarillo, holding a coat and fedora below the Camarillo sign, is greeted at the Camarillo Depot on July 20, 1924. This was the first of three pictures the Arnolds, a husband-and-wife photography team, took this day to commemorate Juan's return to Camarillo after many years living in Argentina. The gentleman in the dark coat with his back to the camera standing in front of Juan is Adolfo Camarillo, Juan's older brother. (Below, courtesy of the Marvel family.)

The Camarillo Depot was unofficially opened on December 15, 1910, and the picture above was taken near that time. According to Juan Camarillo's diary, the first man to buy a ticket here was a guy named Frank Fitzgerald. According to an *Oxnard Courier* article from Friday, December 23, 1910, the depot was officially opened. The article went on to say, "The new depot at Camarillo has at last been officially opened for business. Station Agent Mills is at his place of duty and the people of the community are very much pleased with the fine new building that the Southern Pacific has seen fit to give this growing community." (Above, courtesy of the Marvel family.)

The above c. 1960 photograph shows the Camarillo Depot right after a hail storm. This picture was taken after the depot was moved from its original location in order to construct the 101 Freeway overpass, which was finalized in 1954. The overpass is in the background where the depot originally stood. (Above, courtesy of the Marvel family.)

Carmen Camarillo, Adolfo's youngest daughter, is aboard a white Arabian horse, Pepe, for the 1965 parade at right. The children are, from left to right, Bruce Parker, Ynez Parker LaDow, and Victoria Nicholson. Chico is the name of the Shetland pony pulling the children. Molly Krebs is in the background aboard a horse with an unknown name. (Right, courtesy of the Marvel family.)

The east-facing image of Ventura Boulevard below was taken during the construction of the 101 Freeway in early 1954 near the Glenn Drive intersection. On the right in front of the parked cars, one can partially see Dizdar Park—where a lone tree and bench are standing. The one-story building directly behind the tree and bench is the city's first fire station, built in 1941. Looming above the fire station is St. Mary Magdalen Catholic Chapel. (Below, courtesy of California Highways and Public Works.)

Above is another east-facing image of Ventura Boulevard taken in 1954 during the construction of the 101 Freeway with the Elm Drive intersection on the immediate right. The row of palm trees in the center of the road served as a barrier between what was once the 101 Highway through town (left two lanes) and the service road to the right of the trees. Pleasant Valley Church is on the left behind the Chevron sign. (Above, courtesy of California Highways and Public Works.)

Pleasant Valley Baptist Church, Camarillo, Calif.

The location of the c. 1940 image above of the Pleasant Valley Church is at the northeast corner of Arneill Road and Ventura Boulevard. The road immediately in front of the church is the 101 Highway, which was the route through Camarillo via Ventura Boulevard. The palm tree seen on the right was one of many in the middle of Ventura Boulevard, the other side of which was a frontage road used for local traffic. (Above, courtesy of Florida Baptist Historical Society.)

Ralph Cawelti (pronounced *Call-Tee*) opened Ralph's Service, his Mobil gas station, on Ventura Boulevard in 1954. The white building to the right of the Mobil gas station is the Pleasant Valley Baptist Church, on the corner of Ventura Boulevard and Arneill Road—a full half mile away. (Below, courtesy of Ruth Ann Cawelti Basham.)

The Flying Red Horse stands immediately behind Ralph's Service on Ventura Boulevard in the 1954 image below. The little boy on the red horse is Andrew Cawelti, Ralph's son. Directly behind Andrew (to the north) is the 101 Freeway, running right and left. The street running perpendicular with the 101 Freeway is Mobil Avenue. The walnut orchard at top left is now known as Broadmare Estates. (Below, courtesy of Ruth Ann Cawelti Basham.)

The above view of Ralph's Service on Ventura Boulevard was taken in 1954 from Oak Street. It would be a full 10 years before Camarillo would become an incorporated city. Just look at all that undeveloped land, which today is buried under concrete. (Above, courtesy of Ruth Ann Cawelti Basham.)

On January 10, 1949, Camarillo residents woke up to four inches of snow, and some of the foothills received a few inches more. It was the last time measurable snow fell in town. To put this statistic into perspective, even Miami, Florida, has recorded snow on more occasions since 1949 than Camarillo. At left, Frank and Catalina Harvey stand next to their snowman in Dizdar Park. (Left, courtesy of Betty-Jo Carnes.)

Below, Adolfo Camarillo is delivering a speech in a c. 1952 Christmas program at Dizdar Park in Camarillo. Located on Ventura Boulevard at the corner of Glenn Drive, Dizdar Park was once known as Pleasant Valley Cemetery. It was decided to turn the cemetery into a park with land donated by Mike Dizdar, a Yugoslavian immigrant who paid to move 100 bodies in 1941. Most of the bodies were moved to Ivy Lawn Cemetery in Ventura, but some were left behind because families could not be located. (Below, courtesy of the Marvel family.)

Moses the camel is being led west on Ventura Boulevard in front of what is now Camarillo Plumbing and Paint during the 1955 Lima Bean Festival. Not long after the picture below was taken, Moses made a jailbreak. He was finally lassoed and captured a little over a mile later by Meliton Ortiz, top ranch hand of Adolfo Camarillo, but not before he partially destroyed a local farmer's bean field. (Below, courtesy of Shirley Granger.)

In the above south-facing picture of Ventura Boulevard in 1959, Tony's Red Star Nursery is bookended by State Food Market at left and Carmen's Malt Shop at right. Tony's Red Star Nursery is now Tile City, while the building that was State Food Market is now home to Kay's Coffee Shop and Edward Jones Investments. Today, Carmen's Malt Shop is the very popular Dorothy's Chuck Wagon Café. (Above, courtesy of Steve Bailey.)

Around the 1920s, Horseshoe Bend was one of 49 curves along the Conejo Grade, an obsolete section of the 101 Highway in Ventura County, soon to be replaced by a new highway on an improved alignment. A total curvature of 2,067 degrees would be reduced to 367 degrees and the curves to only 12 in number on the new location routing, which opened in May 1937. (Above, courtesy of California Highways and Public Works.)

VENTURA BOULEVARD AND 101 HIGHWAY

The c. 1930 picture below of Horseshoe Bend along the Conejo Grade is facing north. Today, the 101 Freeway travels left to right (east and west) bisecting Horseshoe Bend. Very few remnants exist of the old highway today. However, the crests of the hilltops in the background do line up for a match. (Below, courtesy of the Marvel family.)

The c. 1935 image at left shows one of the 49 curves along the Conejo Grade—101 Highway between Los Angeles and Ventura—which was built in 1912. This stretch of highway was the scene of many brutal accidents due to its steep and sharp turns. (Left, courtesy of California Highways and Public Works.)

On March 24, 1954, the 5.7-mile freeway through Camarillo was opened. During the opening ceremonies held on the new freeway near Cedar Drive, Adolfo Camarillo was the speaker of the day and cut the ribbon as jet airplanes from Oxnard Air Force Base flew overhead. The $3-million freeway that bisected the town would forever eliminate the last railroad grade crossing on Highway 101 between San Francisco and Los Angeles. These pictures are facing west. (Above, courtesy of Pleasant Valley Historical Society.)

Carmen Camarillo, aboard Rico, one of many white horses Camarillo is famous for, is leading a procession of 200 automobiles and local bands celebrating the opening ceremonies of the 101 Freeway on March 24, 1954, above. Carmen is on present-day Petit Street on her way back to the city community center, which was the site of the fire station, justice court, library, and recreation center on Ventura Boulevard. (Above, courtesy of the Marvel family.)

VENTURA BOULEVARD AND 101 HIGHWAY

The 1959 shot of the 101 Freeway facing west was taken at the base of the Conejo Grade, where the Camarillo Springs off-ramp is currently located. Today, this stretch of road through Camarillo is referred to by locals as "The Camarillo Crawl" due to heavy rush-hour traffic. (Below, courtesy of John Spohn.)

All the land in the east-facing image below of the 101 Freeway toward the Conejo Grade from the Santa Rosa Road overpass was owned by Adolfo Camarillo. Camarillo died on December 10, 1958, just prior to when the picture was taken in 1959. Many motorists were taken out by those majestic palm trees, and there was a small uproar when Caltrans widened the freeway and transplanted several of the trees as a compromise. Note the walnut orchard on the right of the freeway. (Below, courtesy of Jeff Hahn.)

VENTURA BOULEVARD AND 101 HIGHWAY

Carmen Camarillo and Adele Hernandez Flynn are seated in the balcony of St. Mary Magdalen Catholic Chapel in the above c. 1950 photograph. Carmen Camarillo is seated at center, dressed in white and wearing a hat while playing the organ. Adele Hernandez Flynn, wearing black and standing beside Carmen Camarillo, is singing soprano. Flynn was the librarian at the town library on Ventura Boulevard, which is now the Camarillo Chamber of Commerce. (Above, courtesy of the Marvel family.)

Pictured from left to right above, Frances Richardson, Adele Hernandez, unidentified, and Josepha Richardson pose at the fountain next to the St. Mary Magdalen Catholic Chapel. The eucalyptus trees in the background line Somis Road. This photograph was taken no later than 1927, as that was the year the Fulton Hotel—background left—burned down. Today, it is an American Legion. (Above, courtesy of California History Room, California State Library, Sacramento, California.)

Louise Baptiste poses alone on the east side of the St. Mary Magdalen Catholic Chapel around 1918 below. Louise Baptiste was the oldest daughter of Mr. and Mrs. Joseph Baptiste, prominent ranchers in Camarillo. In the summer of 1919, she married Marion L. Pitts, who became a successful local rancher, too. (Below, courtesy of Rhett Searcy.)

Louise Baptiste, center, poses with two friends near the front steps of the St. Mary Magdalen Catholic Chapel around 1918 below. The houses behind the ladies were removed just prior to the construction of the 101 Freeway, which began in 1953 and ended in March 1954. (Below, courtesy of Rhett Searcy.)

Louise Baptiste, left, poses on the fountain on the east side of the St. Mary Magdalen Catholic Chapel around 1918 above. The fountain remains in the exact spot it was in 101 years ago. (Above, courtesy of Rhett Searcy.)

At far left above, Eulalia Romero, age 16, sits on the steps of St. Mary Magdalen Catholic Chapel in 1935. Carmen Romero, Eulalia's sister, is sitting third from the left, and Lupe Romero, Eulalia's other sister, is sitting fifth from the left. Note the fountain over Eulalia's right shoulder. A similar drinking fountain is in the exact same spot today. (Above, courtesy of Roy Villa.)

RANCHO CALLEGUAS

Pictured above is the Camarillo Ranch House around 1966. After Adolfo Camarillo's death in 1958, his youngest daughter, Carmen Camarillo, was unable to keep up with the maintenance and repairs of the old Victorian home, so she gave the house to a group of Augustinians, a Catholic religious order. (Courtesy of the Marvel family.)

Below, Carmen Camarillo Jones, Adolfo's youngest child, visits the grave of Sultan, the foundation stallion for a breed known as the Camarillo White Horse. The original site of the Camarillo White Horses' graves was marked by five palm trees due east of Pepper Tree Lane (now the asphalt driveway leading to the Camarillo Ranch's main parking lot) on the west edge of Calleguas Creek. In the late 1990s, a land developer was supposed to leave the five palm trees and build around them. Sadly, the developer moved the five trees slightly south of the original location and built on top of the graves of the Camarillo White Horses. (Below, courtesy of the Marvel family.)

Above, Frank Camarillo, Adolfo Camarillo's only son, is aboard a chestnut stallion just left of center at the stables of the Camarillo Ranch in December 1936. Note the white Arabian horse just to the right of center. Famous the world over, the breeding of these pink-skinned white beauties seems contrary to all rules of animal husbandry in that the white horses were produced by breeding a white Arabian stallion with a black or chestnut Morgan mare. (Above, courtesy of Steve Bailey.)

Above, from left to right beside their Victorian mansion in 1945 are Adolfo and his wife, Isabella; Francisco and Carmen on white horses; and Ave and Rosa standing by the horses. The man behind them on the horse and the man on the porch are both unidentified. This is one of the very rare pictures of Adolfo Camarillo and all his children that survived to adulthood. (Above, courtesy of the Marvel family.)

The Arnolds were a husband-and-wife team of photographers hired by the Camarillo family to commemorate Juan Camarillo's return to Camarillo after a lengthy stay in Argentina. The photograph below is one of three pictures taken by the Arnolds on this day (July 20, 1924), and it perfectly captures the many parties and barbecues the Camarillo family threw for the community to attend. This picture is facing east on Pepper Tree Lane, which is now the main parking lot just north of where the Camarillo Ranch House stands today. (Below, courtesy of the Marvel family.)

Lima beans are being hauled from the base of Conejo Grade to Hueneme for shipment below. The c. 1910 image was taken very close to where Adohr Lane crosses the Conejo Creek today. (Below, courtesy of the Marvel family.)

The picture above of Juan Camarillo's home was taken around 1930. The Colonial Revival–style home was built in 1903 at a cost of $10,000 and was located within a horseshoe throw of where the Maya Linda and Flynn Road intersection is today. In front of the home there was a road known to locals as Juan Camarillo's Crossing, which—to the west—led to the railroad tracks at Somis Road. In the other direction—to the east—Juan Camarillo's Crossing led to the northern entrance of the property of Adolfo Camarillo, Juan's older brother. (Above, courtesy of the Marvel family.)

The above northeast-facing picture showing Juan Camarillo's home was taken on Juan Camarillo's Crossing, the road that bore his name. To the right (east), Juan Camarillo's Crossing ran into Calleguas Creek. From there, at a 90-degree turn to the right (south) and about a quarter of a mile distance, a traveler would be able to enter Adolfo Camarillo's home from the north. Today, this is an industrial section of Camarillo, with Interconnect Systems, Inc., and Camar Aircraft Parts Co. being the closest businesses to this location. (Above, courtesy of the Marvel family.)

Sadly, Juan Camarillo's home burned to the ground on March 22, 1936. Attracted by the fire, neighbors helped move some of the furniture out of the house. However, personal clothing, bedroom furniture, a large collection of a bric-a-brac, and a large quantity of valuables collected by Juan during a lifetime of traveling were destroyed. Earlier that morning, Juan had left Camarillo for Carpinteria, where he attended church and later spent the day with friends. Because the friends had no telephone, Juan did not know of this devastation until he returned home. (Below, courtesy of Emilio Passera.)

Below, on September 9, 1956, Adolfo Camarillo looks on as student body presidents Gloria Stowers and Kerry Dance prepare the American flag. Within minutes, Adolfo Camarillo would raise the flag, officially dedicating the new $1.4-million high school bearing his name. (Below, courtesy of the Marvel family.)

On September 9, 1956, it was very appropriate that 92-year-old Adolfo Camarillo raise the flag on Adolfo Camarillo High School's inaugural day since he donated the 50 acres of land the school is built on. Today, it is difficult to imagine the hills in the background were at one time so bare. This section of Camarillo is known as Mission Oaks. (Right, courtesy of Camarillo Ranch Collection.)

On October 29, 1957, Camarillo High School students, the band, and the Pep Club surprised Adolfo Camarillo at his home by serenading him on his 93rd birthday. The students then presented him with a massive birthday card signed by almost all of the school's 500 students. (Above, courtesy of the Marvel family.)

On January 10, 1949, Camarillo recorded a high temperature of 44 degrees and a low of 28, bitter cold for the area. Below, in front of the Camarillo Ranch House, Manuela Escobedo (left) and Natavidad "Nati" Servin (right) pose in the rare and remarkable snow. Manuela was Nati's niece, and Nati was a long-term servant of the Camarillo family. (Below, courtesy of the Marvel family.)

Carmen Camarillo, Adolfo's youngest child, stands near the bottom of the stairway inside the Camarillo house around 1975 below. Only some minor remodeling of the interior of the home has been done since this picture was taken. (Below, courtesy of the Marvel family.)

The carriage barn just northwest of the Camarillo House also served as a walnut-processing building in its heyday. The c. 1980 picture above shows how dilapidated the building became prior to a complete makeover in the 1990s. (Above, courtesy of the Marvel family.)

Pictured above is Pepper Tree Lane as it looked in the early 1980s. Pepper Tree Lane ran east and west just north of the Camarillo house between what is now Camarillo Ranch Road and Calleguas Creek. Carmen Camarillo's house can be seen at left. Today, this area is an asphalt parking lot, but the bunya bunya still stands. (Above, courtesy of the Marvel family.)

CHAPTER 3

CAMARILLO
SPREADS OUT

Pictured above is Camarillo Heights in 1927, near East Highland Drive and West Loop Drive. Installed in 1924, this water tank was the first one in Camarillo Heights, on present-day North Loop Drive. With commanding views of the Santa Monica Mountains, the Pacific Ocean, and the Channel Islands, Camarillo Heights was—and still is—a very ideal place to live. (Courtesy of USC Digital Archives.)

The 1927 north-facing picture below of Camarillo Heights shows a little girl and gentleman farmer posing with tomatoes, one of dozens of crops that can be grown in the area due to its fertile soil and excellent climate. Row crops are still grown year-round at this location, but the hillside in the background is now known as Spanish Hills, which is filled with fancy homes and a golf course. The produce boxes read Garcia and Maggini Co., a San Francisco–based company that was a processor of fresh fruit, dried fruit, nuts, and honey. (Below, courtesy of USC Digital Archives.)

A man tends to his turkeys in the north-facing view above of Camarillo Heights in 1927. The location of this farm is not very far from where Rolling Pin Donuts sits today on Las Posas Road. At top left, one can see eucalyptus trees, which were a very common sight in the old days, as they were used by local farmers and ranchers as windbreakers to protect against both the Santa Ana winds from the east and the prevailing westerlies. (Above, courtesy of USC Digital Archives.)

The location of the above picture is near the corner of West Loop and North Loop in Camarillo Heights in 1927. The home still stands, though it has undergone some extensive remodeling. The stairs to the home still exist, too. (Above, courtesy of USC Digital Archives.)

The north-facing view of Camarillo Heights below was taken in 1927 not far from where the football field at Cornerstone Christian School is located today at Arneill and Las Posas Roads. The windbreakers at left are eucalyptus trees that partially still exist today. (Below, courtesy of USC Digital Archives.)

The location of the 1927 photograph below of Camarillo Heights is currently at what is now the Mesa and East Loop Drives intersection. The farmhouse at left still stands on Alosta Drive. (Below, courtesy of USC Digital Archives.)

CAMARILLO SPREADS OUT

Above is a classic 1927 view of a farm in Camarillo Heights that shows how sparse and spread out the properties used to be. Some of the oldest homes in Camarillo Heights—from the 1920s—still exist today, though they are predominantly surrounded by modern homes and larger trees that make it a little difficult to visualize what the area once looked like. (Above, courtesy of USC Digital Archives.)

Vons Grocery Store was the first major supermarket built in Camarillo in what was also the first shopping center. Security First National Bank, in the north-facing image above, is now the FedEx building in the Ponderosa Shopping Center on Arneill Road, built in 1963—the same year this picture was taken. Today, Vons has been replaced by a Smart and Final supermarket. (Above, courtesy of Jeff Hahn.)

Below is an alternative angle of the Ponderosa Shopping Center on Arneill Road in 1963, facing southwest. Today, that alley looks almost exactly the same; only the trees are a little bit bigger. (Below, courtesy of Jeff Hahn.)

In the north-facing 1964 image below, taken from the Carmen Drive bridge that goes over the 101 Freeway, it is easy to see the mostly undeveloped land in the Camarillo Hills. Today, Carmen Drive traces the dirt road here all the way north to Las Posas Road and is a major artery in town. Also, at the end of the dirt road and to the left is where Camarillo City Hall stands today. (Below, courtesy of Ruth Ann Cawelti Basham.)

In 1964, Ralph Cawelti opened a second gas station called Cawelti's Mobil at the southwest corner of Carmen Drive and Daily Drive. It was the first business to open in that vicinity. Today, the Cawelti Mobil Service Station is a 7-11. (Above, courtesy of Ruth Ann Cawelti Basham.)

Above, Evelyn Cawelti, wearing a hat, poses with her children beside the Cawelti Mobil on Carmen Drive on Easter 1964. The children are, from left to right, Jennifer, Ruth Anne, Susan, and Andrew. This west-facing image shows the palm trees that were once parallel to the 101 Freeway. The empty land where the trees are at top right would become Griffin Brothers Mortuary. (Above, courtesy of Ruth Ann Cawelti Basham.)

CAMARILLO SPREADS OUT

Ralph Cawelti, left, poses with his son Andrew during the 1964 construction of Cawelti's Mobil on Carmen Drive. In this view facing northeast, the Camarillo Hills in the background are now covered in fancy homes in the Spanish Hills and the Las Posas Estates developments. (Below, courtesy of Ruth Ann Cawelti Basham.)

The 1970 view of Camarillo taken from Corriente Court in Camarillo Heights proves that it was not long ago when row crops, citrus orchards, and eucalyptus trees still dominated the area. This is just a glimpse of one of the many breathtaking views residents get when living in Camarillo Heights. (Below, courtesy of Jeff Hahn.)

CHAPTER 4

LEWIS RANCH
AND CAMARILLO
STATE HOSPITAL

In this picture, taken on the southern edge of Camarillo, an unidentified man sits atop his horse near current-day Howard Road and Conejo Creek. Even after the invention of the automobile, ranchers and farmers would inspect their property on horseback because it was an easier means of travel, especially in the winter after the rains. Roads were almost never paved, particularly on private property. (Courtesy of California History Room, California State Library, Sacramento, California.)

The woman in the white shawl is Carmen Camarillo, youngest daughter of Adolfo Camarillo, at the dedication ceremony of Camarillo State Hospital on October 12, 1936. The woman she is with is Adele Hernandez Flynn. The hospital closed in 1997. California State University Channel Islands was established in October 1998 with the first classes starting in fall of 2002. (Left, courtesy of Cal State Channel Islands Digital Archives.)

Snow covers the parking lot at Camarillo State Hospital on January 10, 1949. It seems just about every other film noir of the 1930s and 1940s mentioned Camarillo, because the antagonist in those black-and-whites was often mentally impaired. In real life, several celebrities, including Charlie Parker and Jonathan Winters, spent time at this mental institution. This has also been a popular shooting location for Hollywood films, including *The Snake Pit* in 1948 starring Olivia de Havilland. (Below, courtesy of Cal State Channel Islands Digital Library.)

The shot below facing west from January 10, 1949, shows Camarillo State Hospital with Round Mountain just behind it coated in up to four inches of snow. The institute's famous bell tower is just right of center. (Below, courtesy of Cal State Channel Islands Digital Library.)

The photograph above shows the hay barn at the Camarillo State Hospital dairy around 1940. Established in 1937, the dairy operated as part of the hospital's rehabilitation program, in which 20 patients assisted some 15 employees in running the operation. The dairy had a poultry plant, a slaughterhouse, and a provision for carrying 600 hogs. By 1956, the dairy had 220 milking cows that produced 1,100 gallons of milk a day, all of which was used at the 7,000-patient hospital. (Above, courtesy of Cal State Channel Islands Digital Library.)

The above east-facing image shows the Joseph Lewis Ranch residence around 1920, just south of Camarillo. Lewis's father, Henry Lewis, was the first person to plant lima beans in North America; Joseph Lewis was the first to plant them in Camarillo in 1899, and by 1901, he had formed a partnership with Adolfo Camarillo that lasted until 1906. By 1913, a total of 75 percent of the world's lima beans came from Ventura County—a good portion of which from Camarillo. (Above, courtesy of Cal State Channel Islands Digital Library.)

The c. 1910 image below shows the Joseph Lewis Ranch standing strong. All of this is gone now, but prior to the brutal Springs Fire that swept through in May 2013, an old swing set from the property was still standing. In addition to planting the lima bean, Joseph Lewis was also a car enthusiast and once used what is now Camarillo Plumbing and Paint on Ventura Boulevard to store his vehicles. (Below, courtesy of Cal State Channel Islands Digital Library.)

The floods of 1938 caused havoc in Ventura County and Camarillo. Although the largest storm that year was only a 10-year event, it prompted the 1944 creation of the county's first flood-control district. The location of this picture is on the old Lewis Ranch along Calleguas Creek, just west of Camarillo State Hospital on Old Lewis Road. (Below, courtesy of Cal State Channel Island Digital Archives.)

CHAPTER 5

PARADES

This c. late 1940s shot captures Camarillo residents throwing a parade as they celebrate Mexican Independence Day. The exact location of this photograph is on upper Barry Street, near the Glenn Drive intersection. Note the Max Riave float that reads "Clothes of Distinction." Riave was an important businessman in Camarillo's early days. (Courtesy of Pleasant Valley Museum.)

Veteran character-actor Walter Brennan served as grand marshal of the Camarillo Christmas parade at least eight times between 1962 and 1973. The west-facing c. 1969 picture above was taken on Ventura Boulevard just shy of the Carmen Drive intersection. Brennan is one of only three male actors to have ever won three Academy Awards. (Above, courtesy of Jeff Hahn.)

In the early 1970s picture below, grand marshal Walter Brennan is traveling north on Arneill Road between Barry Street and Pickwick Drive. Although often cast as a sidekick in Westerns, Brennan was equally adept in comedy—*Support Your Local Sheriff*—and as a villain in *My Darling Clementine*. (Below, courtesy of Jeff Hahn.)

Because Hollywood is so close, Camarillo has always had easy access, luring movie stars to the annual Christmas parade. The 1970 picture below of Buddy Ebsen was taken on Ventura Boulevard, near the Carmen Drive intersection. A terrific dancer, Ebsen was cast to play the Tin Man in *The Wizard of Oz*, but an allergic reaction to aluminum dust in the Tin Man's makeup forced him to leave the production. (Below, courtesy of John Spohn.)

Above is an up-close shot of Buddy Ebsen at the Camarillo Christmas parade on Arneill Road in 1970. At the time of this picture, he was still starring in his most famous role of Jed Clampett from the 1960s hit show *The Beverly Hillbillies*. The Thrifty drugstore in the background is a 99 Cent Store today, and the Camarillo Bowl is currently Harley's Camarillo Bowl. (Above, courtesy of Jeff Hahn.)

Actor Slim Pickens served as grand marshal in the mid-1970s parade above. The picture was taken on Carmen Drive. The California native had been a bull rider and rodeo clown but later starred in movies. Comedy classics *Blazing Saddles* and *Dr. Strangelove* are his most famous movies, though he played an excellent villain in *One Eyed Jacks*, starring Marlon Brando. (Above, courtesy of Jeff Hahn.)

CHAPTER 6

SANTA ROSA VALLEY AND OXNARD AIR FORCE BASE

The Camarillo dairy, pictured here in the 1920s, was located almost precisely where the Santa Rosa Valley Shopping Plaza is today on Santa Rosa Road and Oak Canyon Road. Adolfo Camarillo's first dairy opened in December 1901. He was partnered with J.F. Lewis; that partnership dissolved on December 12, 1907. Eight days later, Adolfo Camarillo began erecting a new dairy—the largest in Ventura County—and by 1909, it was producing 2,400 pounds of butter per month. It was declared by the State Board of Health in 1918 that the dairy produced the finest grade of milk in the country. (Courtesy of the Marvel family.)

The 1960 photograph below is displaying what the bottom of the Norwegian Grade looked like in the Santa Rosa Valley, near the McCrea Ranch. The McCrea Ranch was owned by famous movie star Joel McCrea and his movie star wife, Frances Dee. McCrea and Dee raised their three children here, farmed the land, raised cattle, and lived a simple lifestyle as part of the community. (Below, courtesy of John Cox.)

As late as the 1970s, driving the Norwegian Grade between the Conejo Valley and Camarillo was always risky because of the chance of being delayed by sheep crossing the road. The west- facing picture above from 1961 shows traffic backed up on Moorpark Road due to the sheep. (Above, courtesy of John Cox.)

The above 1961 shot of the Norwegian Grade (Moorpark Road) shows an up-close view of a typical sheep encounter motorists at the time had to contend with. The Norwegian Grade was completed in 1911 and connects Camarillo and the Santa Rosa Valley to the Conejo Valley. (Above, courtesy of John Spohn.)

The east-facing c. 1965 image below of what is now Mission Oaks Boulevard was taken right across the street from the front entrance of Adolfo Camarillo High School. At the time of this picture, that fence marked where Santa Rosa Road used to end. Today, that fence is the intersection of Mission Oaks Boulevard and Adolfo Road. (Below, courtesy of Jeff Hahn.)

The below shot is of Oxnard Air Force Base's main gate in 1968. Originally known as the Oxnard Flight Strip, the base was used for flight training and aircraft maintenance between 1943 and 1947. From 1947 to 1951, it was used jointly by the Army, California National Guard, and Naval Air Missile Test Center. By 1951, it was operating as Oxnard Air Force Base. (Below, courtesy of Patrick Reel.)

SANTA ROSA VALLEY AND OXNARD AIR FORCE BASE

Pictured in the c. 1944 image above of the Oxnard Flight Strip is a General Airborne Transport XCG-16 glider. Located on what is now Camarillo Airport, Oxnard Air Force Base existed between 1951 and December 31, 1969. During the Cold War, the fighter-interceptor base was part of Air Defense Command charged with protecting Southern California against an air attack by an aggressor. (Above, courtesy of California History Room, California State Library, Sacramento, California.)

The housing tract in the foreground of the above c. 1960 picture of Camarillo was called the Capehart neighborhood, an Air Force project that supplied family housing for Oxnard Air Force Base (now Camarillo Airport). Ground-breaking for Capehart was on August 14, 1958. The housing project was constructed on 51.35 acres and was comprised of 72 buildings containing 315 units on nine blocks. (Above, courtesy of Steve Bailey.)

The Capehart Housing neighborhood is pictured below around 1965, facing north on Calle La Cumbre. The base closed down on December 31, 1969, and in 1975, Capehart was acquired by the Navy and renamed Catalina Heights. In February 2008, the last homes of the former Capehart neighborhood were bulldozed. On January 27, 2010, the dedication ceremony of the new Navy Catalina Heights housing took place. (Below, courtesy of Sam Blankenship.)

Discover Thousands of Local History Books
Featuring Millions of Vintage Images

Arcadia Publishing, the leading local history publisher in the United States, is committed to making history accessible and meaningful through publishing books that celebrate and preserve the heritage of America's people and places.

Find more books like this at
www.arcadiapublishing.com

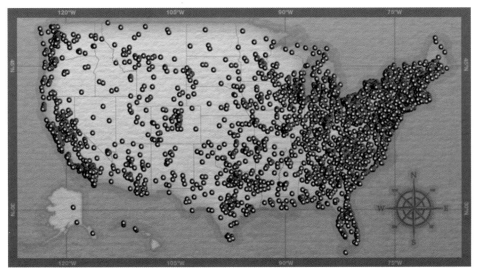

Search for your hometown history, your old stomping grounds, and even your favorite sports team.

Consistent with our mission to preserve history on a local level, this book was printed in South Carolina on American-made paper and manufactured entirely in the United States. Products carrying the accredited Forest Stewardship Council (FSC) label are printed on 100 percent FSC-certified paper.

MADE IN THE USA

PAST & PRESENT

CAMARILLO

David Reel